Heroes and Villains

Stories from Staffordshire Figures

Contents

Introduction 4

Dick Turpin 6

Lady Franklin 10

Mrs Manning 14

Grace Darling 18

William Collier 22

Florence Nightingale 26

The Tichborne Claimant 30

Admiral Lord Nelson 34

James Blomfield Rush 38

John Brown 42

William Palmer 46

Lady Sale 50

Augmented Reality Assets 54

Acknowledgements 55

Introduction

Why would anyone want a murderer on their mantelshelf? Victorian manufacturers of Staffordshire pottery figures produced portraits of a huge range of celebrities. Some, like Admiral Nelson or Grace Darling, were obvious role models. Others were unsavoury characters whose appeal is less obvious.

As literacy increased and newspapers became more widely available, and better communications meant that news travelled more quickly, ordinary people became more aware of what was happening in the world. They wanted to know about the people in the news. The Industrial Revolution meant that more people had a little disposable income to spend on their homes.

From the late eighteenth century onwards, pottery figures of fictional and real people were made in north Staffordshire for sale to ordinary people. They were moulded in two or more pieces and brightly painted. Many have undecorated backs as you could only see the front when they were standing on your mantelpiece. Because they were cheap and made in huge numbers they are not usually marked and it is impossible to tell who made most of them. They are folk art, made by workers for workers, rather than pieces of fine art for rich people.

Their popularity reached its zenith in the mid nineteenth century. Any newsworthy celebrity was fair game and factories often copied engravings from publications such as *The Illustrated London News* to ensure their portrait figures would be recognisable. Heroes of best-selling books, factual or fictional, appealed to the newly literate. National heroes and the royal family were bought by those who wished to show their patriotism; but the Victorian age was one of fascination with the workings of the law, and participants in famous court cases were also popular. Public hangings were regarded as a form of entertainment, and there was a great public appetite for figures based on the protagonists of juicy murder stories. You could buy models of the murderer, the buildings connected with the crime and the chief witnesses, and build up a set to show off to your friends.

Some of the Staffordshire figures are still recognisable today. Others had only a brief moment of celebrity and are now almost forgotten. The twelve stories in this little book reflect the interests of ordinary Victorians and the people they admired or despised.

Throughout this book you can use Layar, an augmented reality app for iOS, Android or BlackBerry devices, to uncover extra interactive content. Download the free app and scan pages marked with the Layar logo.

Dick Turpin
1705 - 1739

During his lifetime Dick Turpin was a notorious criminal: a horse thief, murderer, highwayman and housebreaker. The only mourners at his execution were those he had paid for himself. A hundred years after his death he was famous as a Robin Hood-type hero, thanks to a lurid novel by Harrison Ainsworth and stage shows based very loosely on his career. Audiences wept as his heroic horse Black Bess died after a record-breaking ride to York. But Black Bess never existed, and the ride to York, if it happened at all, was done by another highwayman.

Richard Turpin was born in Hempstead, Essex, in 1705. He trained as a butcher, and his first brush with lawlessness may have been helping to sell stolen deer. He joined the Essex Gang, who specialised in housebreaking with violence. After most of the gang were arrested, Turpin became a highwayman. In 1737 his partner in crime Matthew or "Tom" King was shot during an attempted arrest, possibly by Turpin himself. While hiding out in Epping Forest, Turpin killed a man who tried to

capture him. A £200 reward was offered. He was described as:
"...about 5 Feet 9 Inches high, brown Complexion, very much mark'd with the Small Pox, his Cheek-bones broad, his Face thinner towards the Bottom, his Visage short, pretty upright, and broad about the Shoulders."

Six weeks later Turpin turned up in Yorkshire, using the name John Palmer. He posed as a well-to-do horse trader and lived in Yorkshire and Lincolnshire for more than a year. In October 1738, after he shot a gamecock in the street and threatened to shoot its owner, he was arrested.

Local magistrates doubted that "Palmer" had come by his money honestly. They suspected him of horse stealing – a hanging offence. He was taken to York Castle in handcuffs to await trial at York Assizes.

No-one realised that Palmer and Turpin were one and the same until Turpin wrote to his brother-in-law, Pompadour Rivernall, asking

DICK
TURPIN

for help. Rivernall refused to pay the sixpence postage. The letter was returned to the post office where, in an amazing coincidence, Turpin's old schoolmaster saw it and recognised the handwriting. The schoolmaster travelled to York and identified Turpin, gaining the £200 reward.

Turpin was tried at York Assizes in March 1739 for stealing three horses. He complained throughout his trial that he had not had enough time to prepare, and claimed that he should have been tried in Essex. He was found guilty and sentenced to death.

On 7 April, wearing a new frock-coat and shoes, Turpin was driven to York's gallows in an open cart. He had hired five mourners for ten shillings each. He bowed gallantly to spectators as he passed, and climbed the ladder to the gallows without showing fear. He spoke to the hangman, then threw himself off the ladder and expired in five minutes.

Staffordshire figures of Dick Turpin and "Tom" King were popular, not because of the real Turpin, who was a violent thug, but because of the fictional highwayman dashingly portrayed in stories and melodramas.

Overleaf: *Dick Turpin, attributed to Sampson Smith, Longton, c.1860 [1980.P.267]*

Opposite: *Tom King, attributed to Sampson Smith, Longton, c.1860 [1980.P.268]*

TOM
KING

Lady Franklin

1791 - 1875

Lady Franklin became a byword for perseverance and wifely loyalty because of her twenty-five year quest for her husband's fate. She was also a cultural influence in her own right, especially in Tasmania.

She was born Jane Griffin in London in 1792. Her father was a wealthy silk weaver, and she and her sisters received a good education.

Jane's friend, the poetess Eleanor Porden, was married to the naval officer and arctic explorer John Franklin. In 1825, while Franklin was away exploring the far north of Canada, Eleanor died of tuberculosis. When he returned in 1828 he married Jane. He was knighted in 1829.

In 1836 he was appointed governor of Van Diemen's Land (now Tasmania), then largely populated by transported convicts. He was a relatively enlightened and humane governor. His wife embraced colonial life with enthusiasm, declaring her wish to assist in the creation of an "infant nation". She established a college, a botanical garden and a natural history museum. She offered a shilling each for the heads of poisonous snakes in an attempt to rid the island of them, and tried to improve the welfare of women convicts.

In 1843 Franklin was recalled home. The British government was sending an expedition to chart the North-West Passage, a potential shipping route through the Arctic seas north of America. Franklin was not the first choice to lead the expedition but, even at the advanced age of 59, he was well qualified, having already led three expeditions to the Arctic. Two ships, the *Erebus* and the *Terror*, were fitted out with modern equipment including steam engines for powering through the ice, tinned food and ships' libraries. In May 1845 the expedition set off, with Franklin commanding 110 men and 24 officers, all hand-picked by the Admiralty.

After two years Lady Franklin, alarmed at the lack of news, asked the Admiralty to send out a search party. Because the expedition carried

LADY FRANKLIN

SIR JOHN FRANKLIN

provisions for three years it was 1848 before a rescue party was launched and a £20,000 reward offered. By then Franklin was dead. His body was never found.

Many ships set off to find what had happened to Franklin and his crew. Lady Franklin herself sponsored seven expeditions and campaigned constantly to ensure her husband was not forgotten.

In 1854 the explorer John Rae met Inuit families who had found the bodies of survivors of the Franklin expedition. They sold him relics of the men and told him they had seen evidence of cannibalism.

Rae's report infuriated Lady Franklin. No decent British sailor could possibly have resorted to such an atrocity. In Lady Franklin's eyes her husband and his men were heroes, and she scorned and suppressed any evidence that did not promote this view.

Even after Franklin's death in 1847 was confirmed, Lady Franklin hoped to find his body or further written records. The last expedition she supported left London shortly before she died in 1875.

Thanks to his wife's efforts, Franklin was regarded as a hero in nineteenth-century Britain and Australasia. Lady Franklin was also much admired for her steadfastness and determination; she was known as "the English Penelope" after Ulysses's wife. Staffordshire figures of Sir John and Lady Franklin commemorated this devoted couple.

Overleaf: *Sir John & Lady Frankin, attributed to the 'Alpha' factory, Staffordshire, c.1850 [1980.P.318 & 319]*

Opposite: *Lady Frankin, attributed to the 'Alpha' factory, Staffordshire, c.1850 [1980.P.319]*

Mrs Manning

c.1821 - 1849

The Victorians have been accused of "murder-worship". A murderer was an object of prurient fascination; and if the felon was an attractive woman her notoriety was assured.

Maria Manning was born Marie de Roux in Lausanne, Switzerland, around 1821. By 1846 she was lady's maid to the Duchess of Sutherland's daughter, staying at Trentham in Staffordshire. A lady's maid was expected to be neatly dressed, good at needlework and aware of fashion. Her perks included her employer's cast-off dresses.

Around this time Maria met Patrick O'Connor, a customs officer twice her age. He supplemented his wages with money-lending and seemed like a good catch for Maria. But he dithered over popping the question and in 1847 Maria married Frederick George Manning instead.

Fred was a railway guard who was sacked after a series of train robberies. Maria married him on the expectation of a large legacy on his mother's death. The Mannings' marriage was stormy, and Maria continued to see O'Connor, apparently with Fred's compliance. During a quarrel with Fred, Maria and O'Connor lived as man and wife under the name of Johnson.

After a disastrous attempt at running a pub, the Mannings took lodgings in Bermondsey. O'Connor had promised to rent rooms from them but changed his mind. Fred threatened to sue him and Maria vowed revenge. Outwardly they seemed as friendly as ever.

On August 9, 1849, the Mannings invited O'Connor to dinner. Maria lured him into the kitchen and shot him in the back of the head. Then Fred beat him to death with a crowbar. They stripped him, tied him up and buried him in quicklime in a grave they had dug under the kitchen flagstones. Maria went to his house and stole his money and bonds.

O'Connor was soon missed and suspicion fell upon the Mannings. But Maria had escaped

Maria Manning

F. G. Manning

to Edinburgh, with most of the loot, and Fred took what was left to Jersey. When the police searched the house they noticed that the mortar between the kitchen flagstones was still damp. O'Connor's body was identified by his false teeth.

Maria was arrested after she tried to cash in the stolen bonds and Fred was arrested in Jersey.

At their trial at the Old Bailey each blamed the other, but both were found guilty of murder and condemned to be hanged on November 13. Maria was compared to Lady Macbeth, partly because of her gender, and partly because she was obviously the stronger character. One witness recalled Fred saying: *"For God's sake never marry a foreigner. She will be the ruin of you."*

Maria was described as:
"5 feet 7 inches high, stout, fresh complexion, with long dark hair, good looking, scar on the right side of her chin... dresses very smartly, and speaks broken English."

Maria tried to kill herself before the execution, and refused to see Fred until the night before they died, when they were reconciled. Even in the condemned cell she sewed new underwear for herself and altered her dress to flatter her fine figure. She insisted on wearing silk stockings, rather than cotton, to her execution, and her smart dress was credited with making black satin unfashionable.

Thousands of people, including Charles Dickens, who was disgusted by the crowd's uncivilised behaviour, came to see the Mannings hanged at Horsemonger Lane Gaol. Maria met her death with composure, unlike Fred, whose legs would barely support him, or William Calcraft, the hangman, who was distressed at having to hang a married couple.

Despite their squalid lives and sordid deaths, the Mannings became posthumous celebrities. Maria in particular was the object of salacious interest because of her good looks, striking figure and fastidious dress.

Overleaf: *Maria & Frederick Manning, Staffordshire, c.1849 [1982.P.452 & 453]*

Opposite: *Maria Manning, Staffordshire, c.1849 [1982.P.452]*

Grace Darling

1815 - 1842

Grace Horsley Darling was the ideal Victorian heroine. Brave, feminine, modest, pious and dead at 26, she embodied all the virtues the sentimental Victorians looked for in their womenfolk.

Her father, William, was a lighthouse keeper on the Farne Islands. Grace was the seventh of nine children. She was educated at home by her parents and learned at an early age to handle a boat.

On the night of September 5, 1838, Grace was alone with her parents in the Longstone lighthouse. There was a terrible storm and they could not sleep. In the early hours of the morning Grace saw from her window that a ship was wrecked on the neighbouring Harcar Rock. This was the *Forfarshire*, a paddle steamer carrying passengers and cargo from Hull to Dundee. It was not until dawn that Grace saw survivors on the rock through her telescope.

William knew that the weather was too bad for the local lifeboat to launch, but he could not manage his rowing boat by himself in the storm. Grace offered to go with him.

When they reached the rock they realised that there were nine survivors and they would have to make two trips. While Grace steadied the boat in the stormy sea William helped the survivors. They took five back on the first trip including two of the *Forfarshire's* crewmen, to help with the boat, and a Mrs Dawson, who had to leave the bodies of her children behind. Then William and the two crewmen returned for the rest of the survivors. The whole rescue took just two hours.

At last the lifeboat struggled across to the island. Its seven-man crew included Grace's youngest brother. But the storm was too bad for it to return to the mainland. So there were nineteen people trapped on a tiny island in terrible weather, with only enough food for three and not enough shelter or warm clothing. The storm did not die down enough for the lifeboat to leave for three days.

Grace Darling

News of the daring rescue spread quickly
and was picked up by local and national
newspapers. The idea of the plucky young girl
risking her life to save strangers caught the
public imagination. The equally heroic feats of
William and the lifeboat crew were side-lined.
Grace became a celebrity.

She received hundreds of letters asking for
locks of her hair or scraps of the dress she
wore during the rescue. Artists queued up to
paint her portrait; according to family legend
her sister Betsy sometimes pretended to be her
and sat for the portraits. Even Queen Victoria
sent her £50.

The Duke of Northumberland became
her guardian to protect the unworldly and
innocent Grace from exploitation by showmen
and journalists. She was never comfortable
with her fame and became very reserved.

Grace died of tuberculosis in October 1842.
She was already an icon of Victorian heroism,
and romanticised portraits, novels and plays
ensured that her fame outlived her.

Overleaf: & Opposite: *Grace Darling,
Staffordshire, c. 1840 [1980.P.294]*

William Collier

c.1831 - 1866

William Collier was not immortalised as a Staffordshire figure because of any great deeds, or even misdeeds. His uneventful life and brief moment of criminal notoriety would not have been enough to single him out. It was the unfortunate manner of his death which captured the Victorian imagination and earned him a place on the nation's mantelpieces.

In 1866 Collier was about 35, living with his wife and at least seven children on a farm near Kingsley. He was well known locally as a poacher. Early one morning he took his shotgun and set off for the nearby village of Whiston, intending to pot a few rabbits or pheasants. He was discovered by 24-year-old Thomas Smith, who was a gamekeeper on his father's land at Whiston Eaves. A shot was fired and Thomas fell to the ground. Collier made sure of his silence by beating him to death with his gunstock.

When Thomas's body was discovered shortly after breakfast, suspicion fell straight away on Collier, who was arrested and sent to Stafford Gaol. He protested his innocence but a gun found hidden in a drain was identified as Collier's by the man who had sold it to him. The ramrod was found near Collier's home.

Collier's lawyer tried to pin the blame on passing gypsies. In vain he spoke of Collier's wife and many children. Collier was found guilty and sentenced to death by hanging.

The date of the execution was fixed for August 7th. By the previous evening the rope had not arrived. Usually the rope was a perk for the hangman, who could sell it off by the inch as lucky charms – "money for old rope". Even if it survived, no-one could be sure that it was not frayed, stretched or otherwise weakened; so a new rope was needed for each hanging. The prison officers found the rope which had been used for another execution five months before, and tried to repair it. Eventually the new rope was delivered at half past eight in the evening; but for some reason the hangman, George "Throttler" Smith, decided

to use the recycled rope.

The next morning a crowd of 2,000 had gathered to see William Collier die. Smith wore his customary working uniform of a white smock-frock and black top hat. Like most hangmen of the day he used the short-drop method: the condemned man fell about two feet through a trapdoor and was strangled by his own weight.

Collier was accompanied onto the scaffold by a Roman Catholic priest. He was quiet and compliant as Smith put the noose and hood over his head, and, though pinioned, shook Smith's hand. Smith pulled the lever and there was a gasp of horror from the crowd as the rope slipped off the gallows cross-beam and slithered into the pit after Collier. Poor Collier was dazed but conscious, with livid rope-marks around his neck. The priest was distraught. Collier was brought back up onto the scaffold and the new rope was fetched and tied onto the gallows. Collier had to go through the whole terrible sequence again. This time he was hanged successfully.

This was the last public execution at Stafford Gaol. Several botched executions and the disrespectful levity of the crowds who attended them persuaded the authorities to carry out later hangings in private. Victorian ghoulishness, however, was not so easily quashed. This was a time when it was natural for nursemaids to take their charges to houses where murder had been committed as a treat. What better way to commemorate the novelty of hanging the same man twice than to buy a Staffordshire ornament showing the otherwise unremarkable crime for which he was condemned?

***Overleaf & Opposite:** William Collier and Thomas Smith, Staffordshire, c.1866 [1971.P.6]*

Florence Nightingale

1820 - 1910

The sentimental image of Florence Nightingale as the Lady of the Lamp overshadows the fact that she was one of the most influential women of the nineteenth century.

She was born in Italy in 1820 and named after the city of her birth. Her family was wealthy and she was educated at home in Hampshire. She was charming and attractive, and her parents expected her to make a good marriage; but in her teens she felt that God was calling her to serve mankind, and decided to become a nurse. Her parents were appalled. Women of her social standing did not work, especially not in nursing, which was not then regarded as a skilled profession. Although Florence at first bowed to her family's wishes she despised the parasitic lives led by Victorian women, including her mother and sister, and from 1844 she began to study nursing seriously. In 1850 she spent some time at a religious nursing clinic in Germany, and three years later she became superintendent of the Institute for the Care of Sick Gentlewomen in

Harley Street, London. Thanks to a generous allowance from her father she did not have to worry about earning a living.

Britain entered the Crimean War against Russia in 1854. It was the first war to be extensively reported in newspapers. With the arrival of the telegraph, a correspondent's report could be on his editor's desk within a day or two. Readers in Britain were shocked by accounts of the dreadful conditions in which wounded soldiers were treated. Florence assembled a group of 38 trained nurses, including Catholic nuns, and went out to Scutari, near Istanbul.

Injured soldiers at Scutari barracks were far more likely to die of disease than from their wounds, and there was no proper provision for feeding them. Florence believed that most of the deaths were caused by poor nutrition and overcrowding. Like most people of her time she did not really understand that germs caused infection. It was not until six months after she arrived, when the sewers were

MISS
NIGHTINGALE

cleaned out, that the death rate at Scutari began to drop, and she realised how important good hygiene was. A report in The Times described her as:

"...a 'ministering angel'..., and as her slender form glides quietly along each corridor, every poor fellow's face softens with gratitude at the sight of her. When all the medical officers have retired for the night and silence and darkness have settled down upon those miles of prostrate sick, she may be observed alone, with a little lamp in her hand, making her solitary rounds."

She had become an icon of her age.

On her return to Britain Florence was revered as a heroine. A fund was set up to enable her to establish the Nightingale Training School at St Thomas's Hospital in London in 1860. Although she suffered from depression and was often confined to bed, possibly as a result of contracting brucellosis in the Crimea, she continued to work hard. Her book *Notes on Nursing* was the first real nursing textbook and her work on hospital reform and planning revolutionised health care across the world. She had always been good at mathematics and showed a particular gift for explaining statistics, developing pie charts to illustrate her reports on military health.

By the time Florence died at the age of ninety she had published many works and received many honours. She could be difficult, prickly and snobbish, domineering towards working-class nurses and unsupportive of women's rights, and she was not above using feminine wiles to get her own way; but she was responsible for a great leap forward in the care of the sick for which we are all still grateful.

Overleaf & Opposite: *Florence Nightingale, attributed to Sampson Smith, Longton, c.1860 [1980.P.162]*

The Tichborne Claimant

c.1821 - 1849

The British public has always loved a mystery. Spice it up with a dramatic court case and a long-lost heir and you have one of the greatest sensations of the Victorian age.

Roger Charles Doughty Tichborne's family were baronets and lords of the manor of Tichborne in Hampshire. His parents' marriage was unhappy and he was brought up by his French mother in Paris. During visits to Tichborne Park, Roger fell in love with his cousin but her parents would not consent to marriage. In 1853, when he was 24, Roger left for South America. The following year the ship he was travelling on was wrecked off Brazil. He was eventually presumed dead.

Roger's mother, encouraged by clairvoyants, continued to hope that her son was still alive. She advertised for information about his fate. In 1865 news came that Roger had been found. He was working as a butcher in Wagga Wagga, in Australia. Although he called himself Thomas Castro he owned a pipe bearing Roger's initials. Former servants of the family claimed to recognise him and Lady Tichborne sent money to bring him and his family to England.

Lady Tichborne immediately recognised him as her son. There was a facial resemblance – both had large, soulful eyes and long faces – but Roger had been a slender young man and "Castro" was nearly 20 stone (and continued to grow). "Castro" neither spoke nor understood French, which was Roger's first language, and could not distinguish Latin and Greek. He did not recognise most of his Tichborne relations and they dismissed him as an imposter. Their enquiries suggested that "Castro" was really Arthur Orton, originally from Wapping in London. As far as Lady Tichborne was concerned, however, her son had returned from the dead. She provided him with an income of £1,000 a year.

When Lady Tichborne died in 1868 Orton supported himself by selling Tichborne Bonds for £100 each, which he would repay with interest when he came into his inheritance.

SIR·R·TICHBORNE

Orton brought a civil court case to eject Tichborne Park's tenant, which he hoped would establish him as Roger Tichborne.

Orton was supported by some of Roger's former servants and army friends. He had an unusual genital malformation which Roger may also have had. One of Roger's schoolfriends testified that he had tattoos, which Orton did not. The case was thrown out and in 1873 Orton was tried for perjury under the name of Thomas Castro. The trial lasted nearly a year. "Castro" was found guilty and declared to be Arthur Orton. He was sentenced to 14 years' imprisonment.

The trial generated enormous public interest, partly because of the dramatic style of Orton's counsel, Edward Kenealy, and partly because of Orton's own appearance. His vastly corpulent figure, over 25 stone, was easily caricatured and he became a celebrity. Many people were sympathetic to his cause, paradoxically because he seemed to be a working-class man fighting against the establishment. His followers even launched newspapers in support of his cause.

His subsequent attempts at earning a living all failed. In 1895 he published, for money, a confession in which he admitted to being Arthur Orton; otherwise he always insisted that he was Roger Tichborne. When he died in 1898 his coffin bore the name Roger Charles Doughty Tichborne, though he was buried as a pauper.

The true identity of the Tichborne Claimant will never be known for certain. Perhaps he had convinced himself that he really was Roger. Whether he was an oversized figure of fun or a symbol of the oppressed lower classes he took the secret of his identity to the grave.

Overleaf & Opposite: *The Tichborne Claimant, attributed to Sampson Smith, Longton, c.1873 [1980.P.275]*

Admiral Lord Nelson

1758 - 1805

Horatio Nelson embodied all the virtues of the ideal naval commander. Charismatic, quick-witted and with great personal courage, he was adored during his lifetime and is still revered today as one of Britain's greatest national heroes. However, he could be vain and silly, he often disregarded authority, and his private life shocked even his admirers.

He was born in 1758, one of eleven children of the rector of Burnham Thorpe, Norfolk. When he was twelve he went to sea as a midshipman on the *Raisonnable*, captained by his uncle, Maurice Suckling. He decided on a naval career even though he suffered from sea-sickness all his life. In 1773 he joined an expedition to the Arctic, during which he attempted to kill a polar bear so that he could give its skin to his father.

After action in the American War of Independence he went to the West Indies where he met and married Fanny Nisbet. They returned to live in Norfolk until war broke out with France in 1793. Nelson, in command of *HMS Agamemnon*, sailed to the Mediterranean. In Naples he met the British ambassador, Sir William Hamilton, and his wife Emma. He was blinded in the right eye while taking Corsica from the French, although he never wore an eye-patch. After the Battle of Cape St Vincent, during which he disobeyed orders but personally captured two ships, he was knighted and promoted to rear-admiral.

Shortly after, in Tenerife, he lost his right arm and was invalided home. He was never comfortable writing with his left hand and continued to feel pain in his missing arm.

After defeating the French at the Battle of the Nile he renewed his friendship with Lady Hamilton in Naples. By the time he returned to London his marriage had broken down. He was living in a *ménage à trois* at his house in Merton with the Hamiltons and at the beginning of 1801 Lady Hamilton gave birth to Nelson's daughter, Horatia. Nonetheless London hailed him as a hero.

He defeated the Danes at the Battle of Copenhagen, partly by holding a telescope to his blind eye and pretending not to see a signal commanding him to withdraw.

When war broke out again Nelson was given *HMS Victory* as his flagship. He was now commander-in-chief of the Mediterranean fleet, a vice-admiral, a viscount and a baronet. As he boarded the Victory well-wishers knelt to him and blessed him. The fleet headed towards Cape Trafalgar, on the south-west coast of Spain. Nelson, banking on the French using an old-fashioned linear formation, planned to punch his way through the French fleet, preventing the French from firing broadsides. Early on the morning of 21 October 1805 Nelson made his will. He gave orders to fly the signal, "England expects that every man will do his duty." Thomas Hardy, the *Victory*'s captain, suggested that he change his coat for a less conspicuous one without medals on, but he refused.

The battle was hard fought and there were many casualties. Shortly after one o'clock, a French sniper shot Nelson through the spine and he was carried below. Hardy told him that the French were surrendering. Nelson asked him to look after Lady Hamilton and then said, "Kiss me, Hardy." Hardy kissed him on the cheek and forehead. "Thank God I have done my duty," and "God and my country" were Nelson's last words.

His body was pickled in brandy to preserve it on the voyage back to England. He was given a state funeral and buried in St Paul's Cathedral.

Despite his victory over the French, there was enormous public grief at Nelson's death, though Lady Hamilton and her daughter were ignored and Lady Hamilton was not even allowed to attend Nelson's funeral.

He was adored by the British public and worshipped by his men. But he was conceited and arrogant; he treated his wife appallingly; and while at Naples he had enemy prisoners executed even though he had promised them safe conduct. Nonetheless Nelson remains Britain's most admired naval hero.

Overleaf & Opposite: *Admiral Lord Nelson [1982.P.299]*

James Blomfield Rush

1800 - 1849

The Victorians' obsession with murder was surpassed only by their passion for litigation and the workings of the law. A case which combined the two was bound to arouse feverish interest.

James Blomfield Rush was a Norfolk tenant farmer. After his wife died, leaving him with nine children, he employed a governess, Emily Sandford, to bring them up. Emily became his mistress and bore him a child.

Rush was steward to Isaac Preston of Stanfield Hall who was his landlord. The Prestons changed their name to Jermy to strengthen their claim to Stanfield Hall, which is why Isaac Jermy's son was called Isaac Jermy Jermy. Relations between Rush and Jermy were strained after Jermy commissioned Rush to buy Potash Farm for him. Rush bid £3500 for Jermy, then outbid him on his own account. He compounded this perfidy by borrowing the money to pay for Potash Farm from Jermy.

In the autumn of 1847 Jermy evicted Rush from Stanfield Hall Farm for non-payment of rent, and Rush went to live at Potash Farm.

A year later the day approached when the mortgage on Potash Farm was to be repaid to Jermy. Rush was seething with resentment. He enlisted the help of members of another branch of the Jermy family, and coerced Emily into forging papers strengthening their claim and reducing Rush's debts.

On the night of 28 November 1848, after dinner, Isaac Jermy senior stepped onto Stanfield Hall's front porch to take the air. As soon as he set foot outside, he was shot through the heart. His assailant entered the house and shot Isaac Jermy Jermy. The young man fell dead in the hall. Young Jermy's wife and her maid Eliza Chasteney were both injured. The gunman, a peculiar figure in a wig and false whiskers, escaped. Scattered around the crime scene were notes reading: *"There are 7 of us out here…we have come to take possession of the Stanfield Hall property. Signed –Thomas Jermy, the Owner"*.

James B Rush
Emily Sandford

Rush was suspected immediately. He bullied Emily Sandford into providing him with an alibi. When his house was searched his crude disguise was found, along with other costumes including a widow's dress made to fit Rush perfectly. At the magistrate's inquiry Emily Sandford withdrew her alibi and Rush was committed to trial at Norwich.

The trial attracted enormous public interest. Rush insisted on conducting his own defence. Plans and models of Potash Farm and Stanfield Hall were displayed to help the jury understand the crime's geography.

Eliza Chasteney identified Rush as the gunman who had shot the Jermys. Despite his disguise she had recognised his shape and his way of walking. The handwriting on the notes found at the crime scene was identified as his, and the paper was from his account books.

Rush cross-examined Emily Sandford himself. She wept quietly while giving her evidence and Rush spoke to her affectionately. But much of his questioning of witnesses was irrelevant to the case and he rambled on in his defence, apparently trying to prolong the trial. He was found guilty and sentenced to hang.

He was imprisoned in Norwich Castle and hanged there on 21 April 1849 in front of a crowd of nearly 20,000, many of whom had come up from London on a train laid on for the occasion. His death mask was shown at Madam Tussaud's Chamber of Horrors for many years afterwards.

The legal complexities of the case, its elaborate inheritances and frauds, and the desperate murders and woundings all appealed to the morbid Victorians. Staffordshire figures were made, not only of Rush, but of Eliza Chasteney, Emily Sandford, Stanfield Hall, Potash Farm and even Norwich Castle.

Overleaf: *James Blomfield Rush & Emily Sandford, Staffordshire, c.1849 [1980.P.280 & 282]*

Opposite: *Stanfield Hall, Staffordshire, c.1849 [1980.P.283]*

Stanfield Hall

John Brown
1800 - 1859

No-one can doubt that the cause for which John Brown died, the abolition of slavery in America, was a noble one. In his lifetime, however, he was regarded as a fanatic, and modern writers have accused him of terrorism.

He was born in Connecticut in 1800 but his father soon moved the family to Ohio where he opened a tannery. Brown had hoped to train as a minister, but poverty and eye trouble forced him to abandon this plan.

He was married twice and had twenty children. In 1837 he vowed to dedicate his life to ending slavery on hearing of the murder of the abolitionist minister Elijah P Lovejoy by a pro-slavery mob. Although he was hard-working and determined, times were hard and his businesses suffered. He was jailed when he tried to re-occupy a farm he had lost. In 1842 he was declared bankrupt.

In 1846 he moved to Springfield, Massachusetts, where he met leading anti-slavery campaigners and founded a militant group dedicated to helping escaped slaves. He became convinced that there could be no end to slavery without violence.

Hearing of a scheme to grant land in upstate New York to poor black men, Brown bought land there and set up a homestead at North Elba. The land was poor for farming, and he lived there only a few years; but his wife brought his body back there for burial and the homestead is now a national monument.

His sons had settled in Kansas Territory, and warned him of violent pro-slavery supporters who would stop at nothing to bring Kansas into the United States as a slave state. Brown managed to raise funds and weapons on his way to Kansas in 1855. In May 1856 Brown, leading a group including four of his sons – Frederick, Owen, Salmon and Oliver – hacked five pro-slavery neighbours to death. Brown later claimed he did not personally kill any of the men, though he approved of the murders. At the later Battle of Osawatomie, Brown and a handful of militants fought bravely but were

JOHN BROWN

defeated by superior forces, and Frederick Brown was killed.

Brown returned to the east to raise more funds for the anti-slavery cause. For the next three years Brown travelled though America and Canada raising money, training men and planning an armed uprising of slaves.

In 1859 Brown rented a farmhouse near Harper's Ferry in West Virginia. His plan was to raid the Harper's Ferry Armoury, then to move through West Virginia recruiting and arming slaves as he went. Although he claimed that they would only use the weapons to defend themselves he expected the Virginian economy to collapse without slave labour. He was expecting thousands of men to join him. 16 white men, three free black men, one freed slave, and a fugitive slave turned up. Undeterred, Brown went ahead with the plan. The raiders cut telegraph wires and took hostages. When a black railway employee tried to raise the alarm they shot him; the doctor they called alerted the militia. Ten raiders were killed, including Brown's sons Oliver and Watson. Five escaped including his son Owen. The rest were captured.

Brown went on trial in Charles Town, Virginia, on charges of murder, treason against Virginia and conspiring with slaves to rebel. His lawyer argued that he had not personally killed anyone, he had no reason to be loyal to Virginia and there was no real conspiracy, but he was found guilty and sentenced to death.

Supporters across America and the world argued for him to be pardoned but he was hanged on December 2 1859.

Although Brown was much admired by working Britons sympathetic to the anti-slavery cause, some of his American contemporaries thought he was at best misguided and at worst insane. Certainly his actions helped to trigger the American Civil War. In his last letter he wrote:
"I am now quite certain that the crimes of this guilty land will never be purged away but with blood".

Overleaf & Opposite: *John Brown, attributed to Sampson Smith, Longton, c.1860 [1980.P.130]*

William Palmer
1824 - 1856

Murder is especially shocking when committed by a doctor. Doctors understand drugs and they are trusted members of society; and they are only human. Occasionally the temptation offered by motive and opportunity proves irresistible.

William Palmer was born in Rugeley, Staffordshire, in 1824. He studied medicine in London and returned to Staffordshire to practise. He was a ladies' man and a gambler; he had been accused of fraud during his training; and he had no great reputation as a doctor. The first unexpected death associated with him was that of a friend he had challenged to a drinking competition. Palmer was said to fancy the friend's wife.

In 1847 he married Ann Thornton and the following year they had a son, the only one of Palmer's children to survive to adulthood. Palmer's mother-in-law, who had lent him money, died suddenly while visiting him. Then his friend Leonard Bladen, who had also lent him £600, died in 1850 at Palmer's

house. Although Bladen had been lucky at the races his wife was surprised to find hardly any money on his body.

Four more children died in infancy. This was not unusual for the time, though after Palmer's conviction it was suggested that he had poisoned them by dipping his finger in a mixture of sugar and strychnine and giving it to them to suck.

Palmer insured his wife, who was only 27, for £13,000 and she died in 1854. Palmer still had enormous gambling debts and was forging his mother's signature to pay bills. He was having an affair with his housemaid, whose baby also died, and he was being blackmailed by his former mistress. Palmer's brother Walter was a notorious drunk, and Palmer managed to insure his life for £14,000. When Walter died the insurance company smelt a rat and refused to pay.

Palmer was now desperate for money. In November he went to Shrewsbury races with

WILLIAR · PALMER

his wealthy young friend John Parsons Cook. Palmer lost all his bets but Cook won £3,000. While they were celebrating Cook complained that his brandy was burning his throat, and was later terribly sick. He complained to his friends "That damn Palmer has been dosing me." Back in Rugeley Cook took a room at the Talbot Arms across the road from Palmer's house. On 17 November he met Palmer for coffee and shortly afterwards fell ill again. Palmer divided his time between collecting debts owing to Cook and looking after him. A chambermaid who had tasted broth meant for Cook was also taken ill. Cook died on 21 November, screaming that he was suffocating.

Palmer demanded £4,000 from Cook's family for "payment of debts" and they called for an inquest. Palmer tried to bribe the coroner to return a verdict of death by natural causes. He also tampered with the samples of stomach contents. Despite his efforts the jury at the inquest found that Cook had been poisoned and Palmer was responsible.

Palmer was tried for forgery and for Cook's murder at the Old Bailey in London as his case was so notorious in Staffordshire. The bodies of his wife and Walter were exhumed;

Ann's remains contained the poison antimony. Chemists testified that Palmer had bought strychnine, saying it was to poison a dog. Palmer was found guilty of Cook's murder and sentenced to hang on 14 June 1856.

A crowd of 30,000 turned out to see him die. He kept a brave face to the end, asking the hangman, George Smith, if he was sure the trapdoor was safe. He never confessed to murdering Cook, saying only that Cook was not poisoned by strychnine.

Palmer's mother always maintained his innocence, and no modern jury would convict him on such circumstantial evidence. Although he may have been responsible for at least 13 deaths there is no concrete proof against him. He was certainly guilty of fraud, seduction and forgery; but did he deserve the title "Prince of Poisoners"?

Overleaf: *William Palmer, Staffordshire, c.1856 [1980.P.454]*

Opposite: *Palmer's House, Staffordshire, c.1856 [1980.P.455]*

PALMERS HOUSE

Lady Sale
1790 - 1853

Lady Sale was typical of the indomitable women who accompanied their empire-building husbands into the wars and campaigns of the nineteenth century. Danger brought out the best in her, and she became a byword for toughness and resourcefulness.

She was born Florentia Wynch in 1790, in Madras in India. Aged 19 she married Sir Robert "Fighting Bob" Sale and went with him on army postings to Mauritius, France and Calcutta, bearing twelve children on the way. Sale was a brave soldier but a strict disciplinarian whose men hated him enough to plot his murder. He responded by calling them all on parade and having them fire blanks at him. Nobody took the opportunity to load a musket with a live bullet.

In 1839 the First Anglo-Afghan War broke out. The British deposed the Afghan ruler Dost Mohammed and installed a puppet king. Sale was now second in command of a peace-keeping force. He and other officers sent for their families and established a British enclave outside Kabul, Afghanistan's capital. They amused themselves with cricket, hunting and amateur dramatics. Lady Sale created a garden and grew potatoes.

In 1841 Sale was ordered to take a brigade of soldiers to Jalalabad, nearly 100 miles from Kabul. Lady Sale was to follow on with some of the other families. However, once Sale had left, the Afghans rebelled and surrounded and besieged the British settlement. A combination of the incompetence of the remaining British officers and the treachery of the Afghans left the British without supplies. Dost Mohammed's son, Akbar Khan, seized power. He offered the British safe conduct to Jalalabad. In January 1842, 17,000 people left the British cantonment at Kabul.

It soon became obvious that Akbar Khan had no intention of keeping his word. As the British and their followers marched through narrow mountain passes, they came under attack from Afghan tribesmen. It was bitterly cold and the snow was knee-deep. Lady Sale's

Lady Sale

son-in-law, Lieutenant John Sturt, died of stab wounds, and she and her pregnant daughter Alexandrina had to bury him in the snow. Lady Sale herself was shot twice in the arm.

When Akbar Khan arrived and offered to take the British women and children to a fortress for safety, Lady Sale felt she had to accept his offer, even though she did not trust him. Sure enough, it was not long before he abandoned all pretence that they were anything but prisoners. They were marched from fortress to fortress, occasionally stumbling across the bodies of their former companions, who had been killed by the Afghans or frozen to death.

Lady Sale and her fellow captives, later including some British officers, were held for nine months, during which her grand-daughter was born. She ruled her little company with military discipline, leading religious services and insisting on regular flea checks. Anyone whose morale flagged was treated with short shrift.

In September Lady Sale and the officers succeeded in bribing their captors to free them. One of the Afghans brought them guns and asked who would lead the party.

According to Lady Sale's diary:
"I blush to record that a dead silence ensued. Thinking the men might be shamed into doing their duty, I said... "You had better give me one, and I will lead the party.""

Lady Sale's book, *A Journal of the Disasters in Affghanistan*, was published in 1844. The matter-of-fact way with which she dealt with her terrible experiences made it a huge success and she became famous as the "Grenadier in Petticoats". Fighting Bob died in action in 1845 and Lady Sale died in 1853.

Then as now, Afghanistan was a difficult place in which to conduct a military campaign. The complacency of the British army and the incompetence of many of its senior officers made disaster inevitable. Lady Sale's strong character flourished in appalling circumstances and established her as a heroine of the British Empire.

Overleaf: *Lady Sale, Staffordshire, c.1845 [1980.P.152]*

Opposite: *Sir Robert Sale, Staffordshire, c.1845 [1980.P.151]*

Sir R Sale

Augmented Reality Assets

Throughout this book you can use Layar, an augmented reality app for iOS, Android or BlackBerry devices, to uncover extra interactive content. You can also access this extra information outside the app by navigating to the following locations in an web browser.

A **W** tells you that this person also has a Wikipedia entry - search for them at *wikipedia.org*

W	Dick Turpin	*http://youtu.be/6KbXyALq7uA*
W	Sir John & Lady Franklin	*http://youtu.be/WZUdqgj7AvI*
W	Maria & George Manning	*http://goo.gl/Xz3Eaj*
W	Grace Darling	*http://goo.gl/iYSEpG*
	William Collier	*http://goo.gl/z0pIWF*
W	Florence Nightingale	*http://youtu.be/yhX0OR1_Vfc*
W	The Tichborne Claimant	*http://goo.gl/bMn7xU*
W	Admiral Lord Nelson	*http://goo.gl/DUtjRg*
W	James Blomfield Rush	*http://goo.gl/CgvMFo*
W	John Brown	*http://youtu.be/bSSn3NddwFQ*
W	William Palmer	*http://goo.gl/C1l8ZX*
W	Sir Robert & Lady Sale	*http://goo.gl/3n8che*

To hear the book read aloud go to *soundcloud.com/thepotteriesmuseum/sets/heroes-and-villains*

The Potteries Museum & Art Gallery is not responsible for the content of third party websites. AR assets will be accessible via Layar for a minimum of three years from publication date.

Acknowledgements

With the exception of the figure of Smith &
Collier, all the figures in this book are part of
the P D Gordon Pugh Collection and were
purchased with grant in aid from the V&A
Purchase Grant Fund, The Art Fund and
The Friends of The Potteries Museums & Art
Gallery.

Thank you to all who have contributed to this
project:
Research and copy by Cathy Shingler.
Photography and design by Andrew Dawson.

We would also like to thank the following
individuals for contributing their time:
Claire Blakey, Verity Deaville, Miranda
Goodby, Joseph Perry.

Pitkin Publishing
The Mill, Brimscombe Port, Stroud,
Gloucestershire, GL5 2QG
www.thehistorypress.co.uk

© The Potteries Museum & Art Gallery, 2014
Bethesda Street, City Centre
Stoke-on-Trent, ST1 3DW
01782 232323
www.stokemuseums.org.uk

First published 2014

ISBN: 978-1-84165-565-9

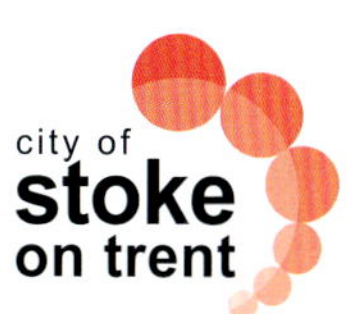